CHICAGO UNLEASHED

CHICAGO UNLEASHED

LARRY BROUTMAN

Ⓑ

BROUTMAN PHOTOGRAPHY, LLC
106 W. GERMANIA PLACE, SUITE 207
CHICAGO, ILLINOIS 60610

Design/editing/production: **Carol Haralson, Sedona, Arizona**
Digital effects: **John Rabias, Chicago, Illinois**
Library of Congress Control Number: 2014931134
International Standard Book Number 978-0-9914502-0-6
Printed in China

The Marshall Field building (now owned by Macy's) was constructed in stages between 1892 and 1914 and contains one of the largest stores in the world. The building is known for the clocks at its southwest and northwest corners.

To my best friend and wife **Susanne,**

who created my interest in and love of Africa

and throughout my photography career served as my best grip, advisor, and critic.

To my best pals and photo assistants, **Shadow and Tanzy,**

who faithfully guarded my car and kept me company on early morning photo shoots.

On their days off they were lent to Mr. George Seurat for some of his more important sketches and paintings.

GLOBAL POSTAL & SHIPPING

Throughout the process of whimsical image making, I was able to rely on the impartial commentary of my editorial staff, Don, Bob and Jumbo Hubert of Global Postal and Shipping. Their facial expressions, or lack thereof, were the best measure of image success. Also, they happened to be quite reliable in getting my hundreds of packages delivered to the various parties involved in putting all of this together.

FOREWORD

Chicago Unleashed is a collection of fanciful photo-generated works created by placing animals within iconic Chicago scenes. The concept originated during the early phase of the design and construction of the Ann & Robert H. Lurie Children's Hospital of Chicago, which opened in June 2012. More than 20 whimsical images, each over four feet square, were created with careful editing and approval by various new hospital committees. These are mounted permanently in elevator lobbies so as to distinguish each floor of the hospital by association with the animal portrayed. The unique creations function as signage and also as pleasing decorative flourishes to enliven and soften the healthcare environment. The images are based on a three-year collaboration between the construction team, directed by Bruce Komiske, Mitchell Associates, which was responsible for signage in the new hospital, and myself as supplier of most of the animal and Chicago photographs as well as some of the final composite images.

This logo identifies images created for the hospital.

Encouraged by the success of the project as measured by the wonderful response from hospital patients, staff, and visitors, I went on to generate hundreds of additional images, taking many more Chicago photographs and greatly broadening the selection of animals to populate them. All the images created for this book were digitally composited by the Photoshop® guru John Rabias. The image selection represents a good cross section of the total images created during the period 2009 to 2013. Captions accompanying the images are designed to be informative, as in a guidebook, but with an occasional tongue-in-cheek twist. — LARRY BROUTMAN, 2013

CONTENTS

Built in 1921 with a six-story-high sign visible for blocks, the French Baroque **Chicago Theater** was one of America's first truly lavish movie theaters. Its grand lobby is modeled after the Royal Chapel of Versailles. It combined stage shows with movies through the 1960s and today hosts concert productions.

Dancing Queen

The 1892 Chicago Historical Society building that once housed Excalibur nightclub is now home to Castle, a dance club with three floors featuring Top 40, Latin, and contemporary "trance" music.

Professional bear walker

The Old Water Tower pumping station was
constructed of large limestone blocks in 1869, which
perhaps explains why it was the only building in the
area to survive the great Chicago fire of 1871.

Amateur bear walker

The Chicago Board of Trade building, built in 1930, is the primary trading

venue for some of the Chicago exchanges. Known for its art deco architecture,

it was for a number of years the tallest building in Chicago. At the south end

of LaSalle Street, it is adjacent to a number of Chicago banks.

Birdman

Symphony Center, a music complex located on South Michigan Avenue, is home to the Chicago Symphony Orchestra. It opened in 1904 in a building designed by the renowned Chicago architect Daniel Burnham.

Urban cowboy

Chicago City Hall is the official seat of government of
the city and was completed in 1911. An imposing neoclassical design, it is essentially a large office building
housing most of the city offices. The building occupies a
whole city block in the central Loop district.

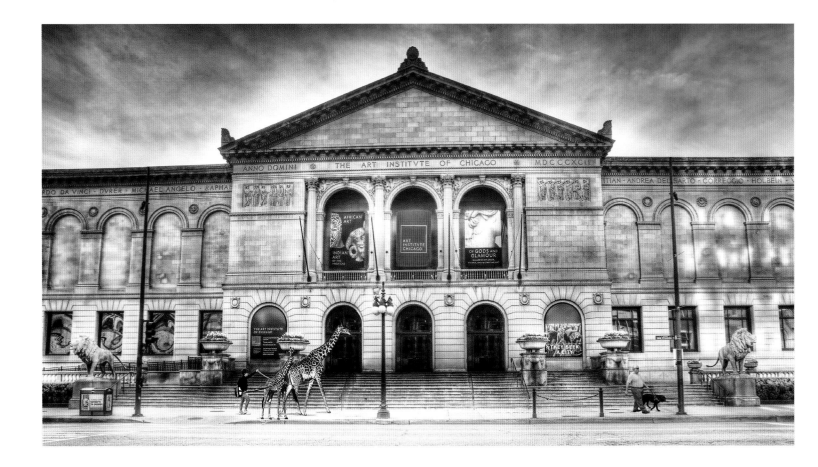

Giraffe Shelter Volunteer

The Art Institute of Chicago is one of the most identifiable

buildings in the city. The museum opened at its current location in

1893 simultaneous with the 1893 World Columbian Exhibition in

Chicago. It is one of the premier art museums of the world.

Lion caught snoozing in "Chicago Savannah."

The Lurie Garden is a 2.5-acre public garden located at the southern end of Millennium Park. A visitor standing on one of the garden's paths can photograph a city skyline with beautiful flower and plant colors in the foreground.

Panda Trainer

The AT&T Plaza is a public space that contains *Cloud Gate*, a three-story sculpture nicknamed "The Bean." The sculpture was designed by Anish Kapoor and is comprised of 168 welded stainless steel plates polished so that the seams are not visible. The resulting highly reflective surface reflects part of the city skyline and also curious visitors who go to extremes to photograph themselves in various poses in front of and under The Bean.

Chicago Mahout

The Clarence Buckingham Fountain of Grant Park, commissioned in 1927 by Kate Buckingham, is one of the most beautiful and photographed fountains in the world. It is the perfect foreground for one of the most beautiful skylines in the world, showing off the elegant architecture of Chicago.

Create your own caption here: _____

ART AND ARCHITECTURE

Alexander Calder's **Flamingo**, installed in front of the
Kluczynski Federal Building in 1974, stands 53 feet tall
and weighs 50 tons. Its beautiful "Calder Red" against the
black face of the Mies van der Rohe–designed building is
easily spotted by our migrating flamingos.

The Chicago Picasso

Pablo Picasso donated this untitled cubist sculpture to the citizens of the city, who simply call it The Chicago Picasso. Made of Cor-Ten steel, it rises in front of the Richard J. Daley Center, whose façade is made of the same material. The sculpture was unveiled in 1967 and is 50 feet tall.

As seen here, not only children enjoy playing on the various facets of the sculpture.

Forever Marilyn

Designed by Seward Johnson, the 26-foot-tall, 17-ton statue depicts Marilyn Monroe in a pose from her film

The Seven Year Itch. It was erected in Pioneer Court adjacent to Tribune Tower on Michigan Avenue and later moved to

a more permanent home in Palm Springs, California. Bearback riders are often seen shopping on Michigan Avenue.

Lions of the Art Institute

The exterior of the Art Institute on Michigan Avenue is adorned

by bronze lions designed and crafted by Edward Kemeys in 1894.

Agam Sculpture

Communication X9, installed in 1983, is located across the street from the Chicago Cultural Center. The 43-foot-high

sculpture is said to resemble a totem pole. It was originally designed by Yaacov Agam, an Israeli artist.

The Chicago Cultural Center, designed in a generally neoclassical style with Italian Renaissance elements, was completed in 1897 and originally housed the Chicago Public Library. One of the interior highlights is a Tiffany stained-glass dome. It is conveniently located directly across from Millennium Park on Michigan Avenue.

The 35 East Wacker Building and Clock, built in 1927 at the corner of Wabash and Wacker, is one of the more handsome buildings in Chicago. Designed into the building at the northeast corner is a beautiful clock with a face surrounded by jewel-like red bulbs and a top that is a statue of Father Time.

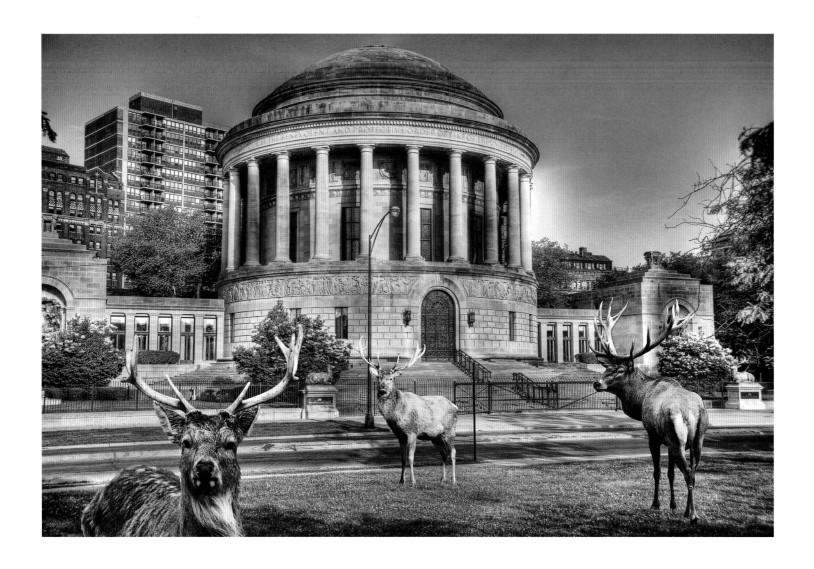

The Elks Veteran Memorial

was dedicated in 1924 and overlooks Chicago's Lincoln Park. The Roman styled Pantheon-like structure has an interior constructed of marble from all over the world. The building was dedicated to the memory of those members killed in World War I.

DuSable Bridge, Wrigley Building, and Tribune Tower

Looking north from the DuSable Bridge, which spans the Chicago River, the Wrigley Building is on the west side of Michigan Avenue and the Tribune Tower is on the east side. The ornate bridge tender houses on the south and north ends of the bridge each have wonderful figural sculptures. The Wrigley Building, built to house the headquarters of the Wrigley company, was completed in 1924. Its glazed terracotta façade gleams bright white, particularly when lit at night. The neo-Gothic Tribune Tower with its ornate buttresses surrounding the tower's peak is home to the Chicago Tribune and Tribune Company. It was completed in 1925.

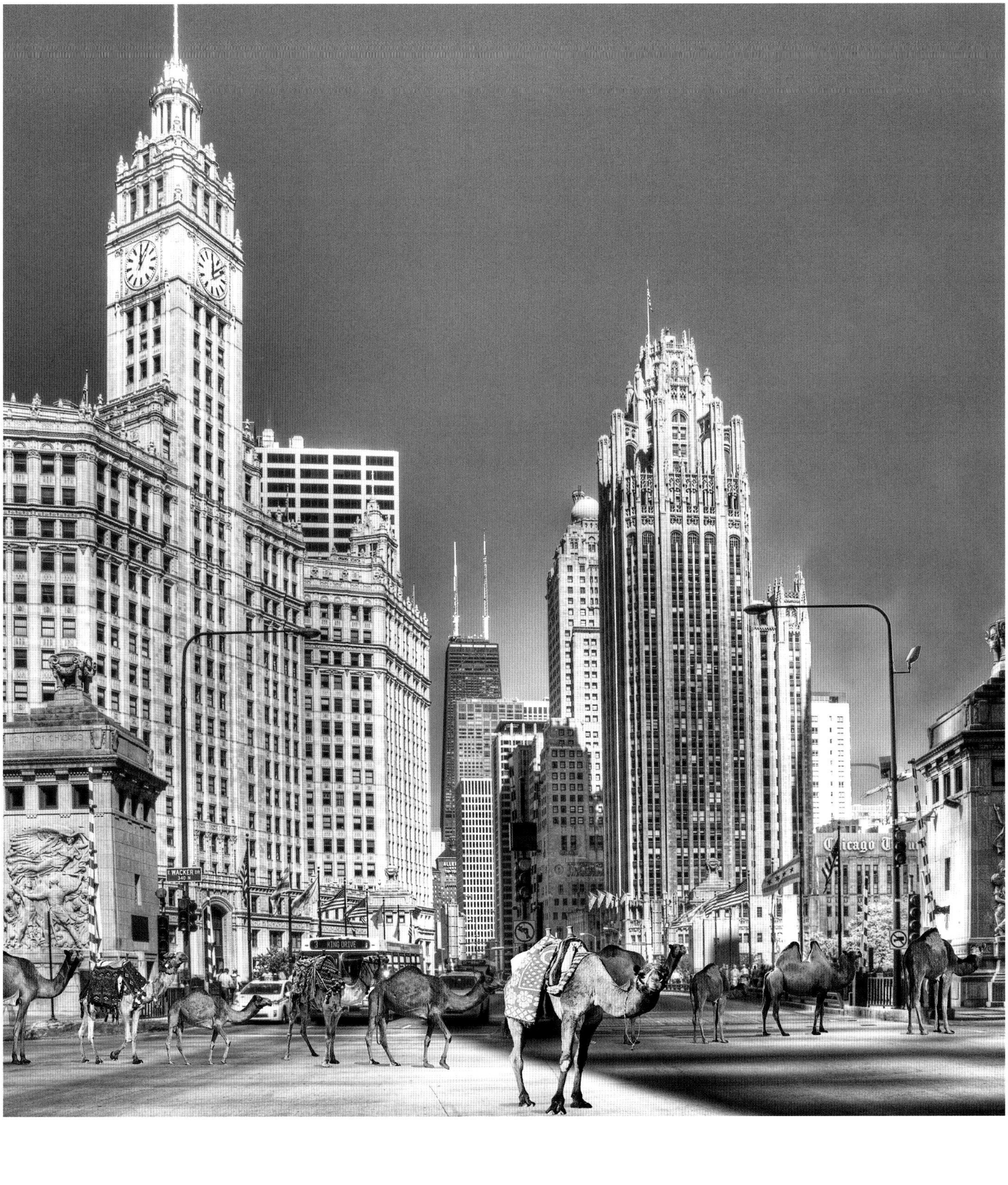
KING DRIVE

Trump Tower and Willis Tower

Prominent on the Chicago skyline when viewed from the north are the Trump International Hotel and Tower and the

Willis Tower to the right (formerly Sears Tower). The Willis tower, the tallest building in Chicago, is readily identifiable.

This 108-story, 1,451-foot-high skyscraper was completed in 1973 and was the tallest building in the world for nearly

25 years. The Trump tower is a 96-story structure housing a hotel and condos. In the foreground are seen a variety of

migrating birds including an Egyptian goose, glossy ibis, and South American parrot.

Wrigley Building Tower

As viewed from the 16th floor of Trump Tower, the Wrigley Building Clock and Tower are

clearly seen along with the Chicago River and Lake Michigan.

Equestrian Indian

Two equestrian Native American sculptures were installed in Congress Plaza (Grant Park area) in 1928 as an idealized

portrayal of Native Americans. The bowman (shown here) and the spearman, each 17 feet tall, were cast in Europe.

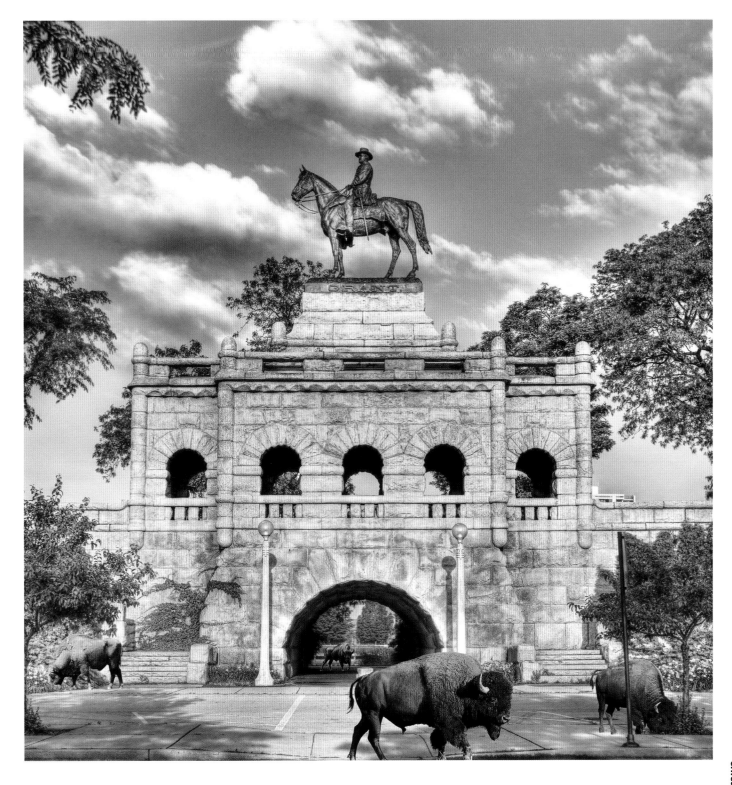

The Ulysses S. Grant Memorial, a bronze sculpture installed in 1891, shows the two-term president as an equestrian. It stands on a massive arched base of rusticated stone in Lincoln Park.

The Bahá'í House of Worship in Wilmette, Illinois, is the only one of its kind in the United States. Construction began in 1922 but the exterior of the building was not completed until 1943. The building is clad with a mixture of Portland cement and quartz and embellished with very intricate carved details that make it beautiful to view at any time of day.

Daley Plaza and the Richard J. Daley Center honor Chicago's longtime mayor. The center was completed in 1965 and houses courtrooms and office space for the city and Cook County. The plaza adjacent to the building is dominated by the Picasso sculpture, but also contains a beautifully lit in-ground fountain and eternal flame war memorial.

Lilies

This Grant Park sculpture was installed in 2008, designed by Dessa Kirk, and is crafted from pieces of Cadillacs from her home town in Alaska.

Chia Heads

A public art display along South Michigan Avenue, sponsored by Plant Green Ideas, stimulates thoughts of the environment. The heads are approximately 12 feet high and accompanied by sustainable plantings.

The Michael Jordan statue, officially known as *The Spirit,* was installed outside the United Center stadium in 1994. Bronze on black granite, it stands 12 feet high on a 5-foot base.

Monument with Standing Beast (1984), by Jean Dubuffet, stands in front of the Helmut Jahn–designed James R. Thompson Center in downtown Chicago. This sculpture is made of Fiberglas and stands 29 feet high.

Statue of the Republic

As originally designed for the Columbian Exposition of 1893, the statue was over 60 feet tall and comprised of gilded plaster. It was destroyed by fire shortly after the exposition. Later reconstructed, but only 24 feet tall, the statue is made of gilded bronze and was installed in place in 1918. The commemorative statue was re-gilded and re-dedicated in 1993. It is known in Chicago as the "Golden Lady."

The Spirit of Progress

One of the original Montgomery Ward buildings, completed in the 1920s, on Chicago Avenue along the Chicago River was capped by a 22-foot statue called *The Spirit of Progress*. While this building is now a residential condominium, the beautiful statue is still maintained in its original position, several hundred feet above the ground.

Agora, the work of Magdalena Abakanowicz, was installed in Grant Park in 2006. Consisting of 106

nine-foot-tall cast iron headless torsos, it is one of the most extensive sculptural installations in Chicago.

The State Street Bridge spanning the Chicago River has been rebuilt at least twice since 1864 and is now a lift bridge, allowing tall-masted boats to move to the harbors in Lake Michigan and back again in spring and fall.

Chicago Reflections

Jet streams and green winged macaws identify up and down elevators on

the public 11th floor of the Ann & Robert H. Lurie Children's Hospital.

Chicago River Walk, on the south bank of the river, offers good views of the surrounding buildings, particularly the Wrigley Building and Tribune Tower.

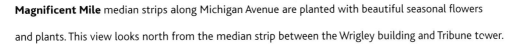

Magnificent Mile median strips along Michigan Avenue are planted with beautiful seasonal flowers and plants. This view looks north from the median strip between the Wrigley building and Tribune tower.

Chicago car wash now offering free elephant washes.

The Chicago El

(elevated) is the rapid transit system serving Chicago and some of its suburbs. Some of the lines operate both elevated and below ground (subway) and the entire system carries nearly a million people a day.

McCormick Place is the convention center for the City of Chicago. The first of the current buildings (not shown here) along the lakefront was designed in the style of a Mies van der Rohe building by a former associate of Mies. The north building, completed in 1996, is connected to the original building on the east side of Lake Shore Drive by an enclosed pedestrian bridge. The south building was dedicated in 1997, and the latest building, the west building, opened in 2007. The Association of Zoos holds its annual convention at McCormick Place.

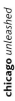

LaSalle Street is known for its office buildings and banks lining both sides of the street as well as the Board of Trade at the south end of the street.

Create your own caption here: _____

In a city like Chicago, it is not unusual to see construction helicopters lifting equipment to the roofs of high-rise buildings.

The Chicago Pride Parade dates to 1970. Currently it occurs in June or July in Lake View East. Attendance along the route can exceed 500,000 and parade participants include politicians, TV and radio celebrities, sports figures, religious groups, and a variety of floats and bands. A spectacular and colorful event.

The 1902 Chicago Fire Station located across the street from the Ann & Robert H. Lurie Children's Hospital is constructed of the same quarry stone as the Old Water Tower. The firehouse has the appearance of a medieval castle.

Illinois senator marches in Chicago's annual gay pride parade.

Navy Pier is a 3,000-foot-long pier on the Chicago shoreline of Lake Michigan. Constructed in 1916, it was intended to serve as a cargo facility for lake freighters and allowed for the construction of warehouse facilities. Navy Pier has evolved into an entertainment, shopping, and dining complex and includes a 150-foot-high Ferris wheel and musical carousel. It is also the starting point for many lakefront cruise ships.

The Carousel at Navy Pier is a colorful attraction.

Metal recycling

On any given day one will find major piles of discarded

metal products on the way to a shredder for recycling.

Also, good pickings for all the local bears.

Streets and Sanitation Department hiring non-union labor.

Missing British tourist last seen near Caldwell Lily Pond.

Caldwell Lily Pond

The Lily Pond, first landscaped in 1889, is a quiet area in Lincoln Park and a good location for bird watchers and those who simply want to enjoy the natural beauty.

Old Water Tower

The Old Water Tower and Pumping Station along Michigan Avenue's Magnificent Mile were built in 1869 and were the only buildings to survive the great Chicago fire of 1871. The old water tower, constructed of limestone blocks, resembles a tiny European castle and the tower is over 150 feet high. The lower portion of the tower is shown here with the pumping station behind. Horse and carriage tours originate from this location, and special arrangements can be made (at extra cost) to substitute a nicely decorated zebra for the horse.

iPad Launch

Any Apple store on the occasion of the launch of a new product can be a busy place. The Chicago store on Michigan Avenue, on the occasion of an iPad launch, had a line around the block.

Chicago Marathon

The Chicago marathon was established in 1977 and is now one of the six

World Marathon majors. Tens of thousands of runners participate.

DINING AND DRINKING

It would be hard to find popcorn products more delicious and original than those prepared at **Garrett Popcorn**, a Chicago original since the 1940s. Although now with shops in other parts of the U.S., Chicago remains its number one location. In Chicago, their long lines are legendary.

The Kerryman is an Irish pub in the heart of the River North area of Chicago. Summer flower displays surrounding the pub enhance the entire neighborhood.

The McDonalds **Golden arches** are one of the best known corporate icons in the world. One of its showcase restaurants is at the corner of Clark and Ontario streets in Chicago. The city is still the headquarters for McDonalds and has a number of its restaurants dating to the 1950s.

Chicago's **Chinatown** is not only a major tourist attraction but a popular area for locals who want to enjoy a delicious Asian lunch or dinner. It is home to over 70,000 residents.

Create your own caption here:_____

("Confused gorilla seen posing at local restaurant" – proposed by Megan Brill, age 11)

The Big Dipper is not a restaurant, but a magical creation invented for one of the elevator lobby floors of the Ann & Robert H. Lurie Children's Hospital of Chicago. The image shows the John Hancock building lit at night with the Water Tower Place condominium to its left.

Steakhouses are the best known dining venues in Chicago. Here, with Trump Tower in the background, at the corner of Erie and Dearborn streets, are two of the most frequented, Keefer's and Harry Caray's.

LAKEFRONT

Montrose Dog Beach at Montrose Avenue and Lake Shore Drive (above and previous spread) offers many amenities, the most popular being accessibility to the water for pets.

Oak Street Beach on North Lake Shore Drive is easy to reach by pedestrian underpass. A concrete path separating the beach and Lake Shore Drive forms a continuous path with beaches on the north and south and provides a running and cycling pathway that extends for many miles.

Oak Street Beach offers watery amusement.

City Council proclaims Chicago River safe for swimming.

Chicago's First Lady Architectural Tours

The Chicago River is one of the most distinguishable geographic features of the Chicago area.

Over 150 miles in length, it has 45 movable bridges linking its banks. River walks are being

added near the center of the city. The Chicago Architecture Foundation and Chicago's

First Lady Cruises offer Chicago River cruises to showcase the world-renowned architecture of

Chicago, much of which can be viewed from the river.

The boat shown can hold up to 200 people on two decks.

Chicago Harbor

This Chicago harbor is just north of Navy Pier and during the summer months is one of the only harbors available for anchoring boats and swimming in the lake. Lake parties are common, and even killer whales don't stop the fun.

Burnham Harbor, a part of Burnham Park, is protected by Northerly Island on the east and is adjacent to the museum campus (Field Museum, Shedd Aquarium, and Adler Planetarium). Views from Northerly Island, the former home of Meigs Airport, provide spectacular images of the Chicago skyline.

The Chicago Harbor Lighthouse is an automated active lighthouse, standing at the end of the northern breakwater protecting the Chicago Harbor and the mouth of the Chicago River. Constructed in 1893 for the World's Columbian Exposition, it was moved to its current location in 1919. The image of the lighthouse is used by The Chicago Lighthouse for the Blind as an identifiable logo.

The Museum of Contemporary Art,
near Water Tower Place on Chicago Avenue,
opened in 1996. Its collection contains over
2,700 objects and includes works of art
from 1945 to the present. The monumental
staircase and street level space often host
outdoor exhibits.

Shedd Aquarium is an indoor public aquarium that opened in 1930. It is one of the largest indoor aquariums in the world and one of the most popular cultural attractions in Chicago. Its location on the museum campus and on the shore of Lake Michigan provides a perfect setting. The oceanarium, opened in 1991, features many marine mammals, including dolphins and whales.

The Museum of Science and Industry is located in the Hyde Park neighborhood between Lake Michigan and The University of Chicago. It is housed in the former Palace of the Fine Arts built for the World's Columbian Exposition of 1893. Established in 1933, it is the largest science museum in the United States.

The Adler Planetarium, on the eastern end of Northerly Island, is part of the museum campus. It was built in 1930 and was the first planetarium in the Western Hemisphere.

The Peggy Notebaert Nature Museum

is located in Chicago's Lincoln Park, not far from the

Lincoln Park Zoo. It is the museum of the Chicago

Academy of Sciences and opened at this location in

1999. The museum focuses on the natural history of the

Chicago region. Near the front entrance of the museum

is a beautiful and realistic bison sculpture.

The new wing of the **Art Institute of Chicago,** designed by Renzo Piano, was completed in 2009, increasing gallery space by 30 percent. The Nichols Bridgeway shown in the background connects the building to Millennium Park.

Mayor delivers on promise to bring East African wildebeest migration to Chicago.

More to the story: East African wildebeest migration: Wildebeest along with migrating zebras and gazelles constantly circulate between the Maasai Mara of Kenya and the Serengeti of Tanzania in an annual cycle based on available grass for grazing. The animals must cross Kenya's Mara River, which is full of hungry crocodiles, and avoid waiting lions on the river banks.

The Field Museum, located in Museum Park near the center of the city, is an outgrowth of the Columbian Exposition held in Chicago in 1893. The opening day for the museum in the current location was in 1921. This museum is one of the finest natural history museums in the country.

The Chicago River

The south bank of the Chicago River east of Michigan Avenue is accessible from the street by different sets of stairs. A walking path provides pedestrians with good views of the river and the boats that sail on it.

The Lincoln Park Lagoon directly east of Lincoln Park Zoo is home to geese and ducks and is also used by rowers in various size shells.

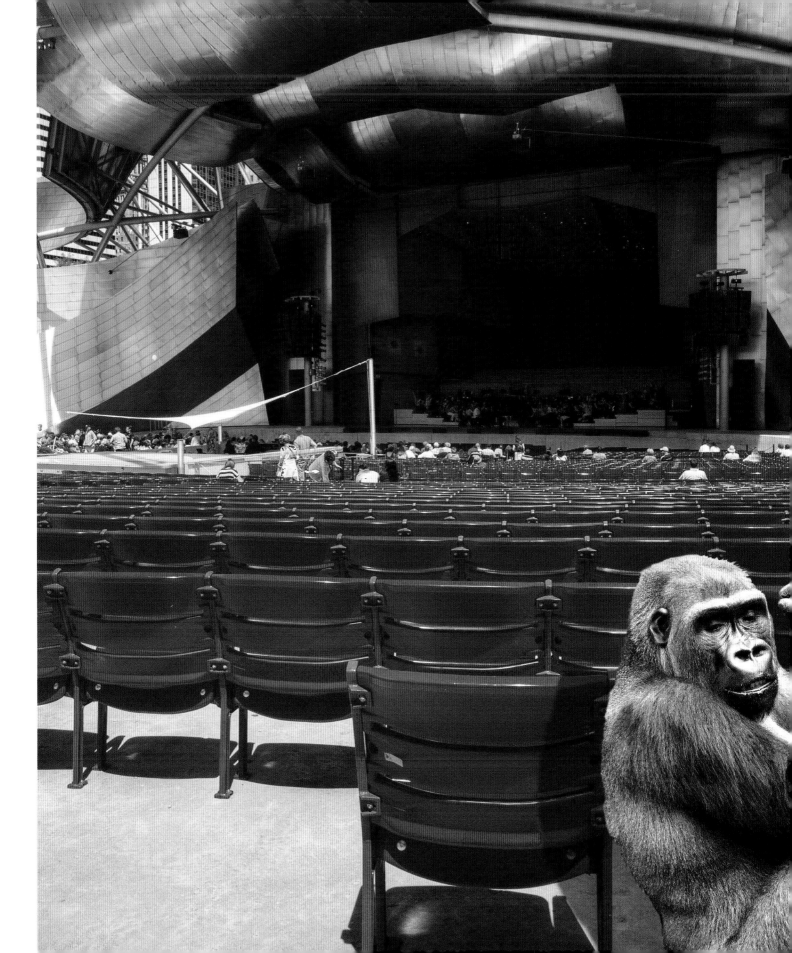

Parks & Gardens

Jay Pritzker Pavilion

Millennium Park is a public park located in the Loop area of Chicago. Construction began in 1998 and the park was completed in 2004 at a cost of approximately 500 million dollars. It is part of the 300-acre Grant Park and features the Crown fountain, the Lurie Garden, Cloudgate, the BP Pedestrian bridge, and the McCormick Tribune ice skating rink. The centerpiece of Millennium Park is the Jay Pritzker Pavilion, a bandshell designed by Frank Gehry that seats 4,000 in fixed seats and 7,000 on the surrounding lawn. Its stage is framed by curved stainless steel plates.

Create your own caption here: _____

Pritzker Pavilion now allows ticket holders to bring pets to concerts.

The Pritzker bandshell is dramatically lit in the evening

and the colors change from a beautiful blue to vivid yellow.

Missing cat found hallucinating at Cloud Gate.

Cloud Gate is a three-story structure nicknamed "The Bean." The sculpture was designed by Anish Kapoor and is comprised of 168 welded stainless steel plates. The highly polished surface encourages visitors to photograph reflections of themselves in numerous inventive poses.

Crown Fountain, designed by artist James Plensa, is a black granite reflecting pool with transparent glass brick fountain towers, 50 feet high, at both ends. The towers use light-emitting diodes behind the bricks to display digital videos. The videos shown are mostly faces of Chicago citizens. Water cascades down the tower tops and the videos are timed to have water spouting out of puckered mouths. The fountain is a public play area and on hot days hundreds of families with small children are seen splashing in the fountains.

Lurie Garden is a 2.5-acre public garden located at the southern end of Millennium Park. From one of the garden paths one can photograph the city skyline with the beautiful flower and plant colors in the foreground.

Chicago Botanic Garden, located in the northern suburb of Glencoe, is a 385-acre property featuring 26 display gardens and a substantial pond. It opened in 1972. The gardens include a bonsai collection, English walled garden, rose garden, and prairie landscapes.

Chicago engineer finds new way to weight-test pedestrian bridges.

BP Pedestrian Bridge is a footbridge over Columbus Drive

that connects Millennium Park to the Maggie Daley Park.

The bridge was designed by Frank Gehry and is in harmony with the

Gehry-designed bandshell with its stainless steel exterior panels.

The Lincoln Park Conservatory

adjacent to the Lincoln Park Zoo was constructed in the 1870s. A formal garden was added a short time later. Continued improvements over the years have included a beautiful fountain surrounded by gardens planted each year with colorful annuals.

City Hall Rooftop Garden

Chicago's most famous roof garden tops City Hall. First planted in 2000, it was part of a demonstration project to test the benefits of green roofs. It is believed that green roofs reduce stormwater runoff, filter air, provide roof insulation, and of course add beauty to the city. There are now more than 200 green roofs in Chicago.

City Hall
Roof

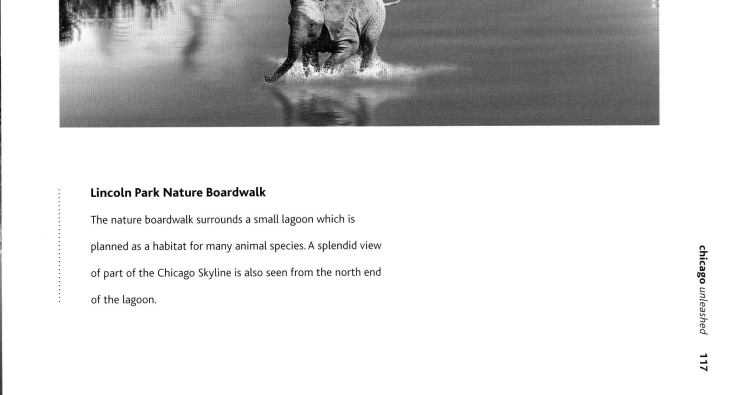

Lincoln Park Nature Boardwalk

The nature boardwalk surrounds a small lagoon which is
planned as a habitat for many animal species. A splendid view
of part of the Chicago Skyline is also seen from the north end
of the lagoon.

Create your own caption here: _____

WINTER

McCormick Tribune Plaza and Ice Rink

operates as a multipurpose venue that during

the winter months becomes a free ice skating

rink. It is located on a level below the AT&T

Plaza so the rink appears to be directly below

The Bean.

Oak Street is a short street in Chicago's Gold Coast Historic District and, for one block beginning at Michigan Avenue, a very upscale shopping location. Some of the most exclusive jewelers and boutiques line both sides of the street. During the holiday season the street is as beautifully lit as Michigan Avenue.

Daley Plaza

The Daley Plaza Christmas tree is the city of Chicago's official Christmas tree, a tradition dating back to 1913. In addition, beginning in 1996 a Christkindlmarket modeled after those in Germany takes place in the Plaza from Thanksgiving to Christmas. The market offers mostly handcrafted and unique items.

WRIGLEY FIELD

Wrigley Field is a world-famous baseball venue located on Chicago's north side. It has been the home park of the Chicago Cubs since its construction in 1916. Between 1921 and 1970 it also served as the home of the Chicago Bears of the National Football League. Wrigley is known for its ivy-covered brick walls and the iconic red marquee over its main entrance.

Create your own caption here: _____

BUCKINGHAM FOUNTAIN

Clarence Buckingham Memorial

Fountain between S. Columbus Drive and

S. Lake Shore Drive at E. Congress Parkway,

was installed in 1927. It is probably one of the

most photographed fountains in the world

and certainly one of the most photographed

sites in Chicago. For wildlife photographers,

the amazing variety of animals that play in

and around the fountain create wonderful

opportunities for award-winning photographs.

The Buckingham Fountain was made possible by Kate Buckingham, who donated it in honor of her brother Clarence. When the fountain operates in the summer months, the periodic 150-foot-high water sprays and evening light shows are some of the highlights.

Chicago air show budget trimmed due to government cutbacks.

The Chicago Air and Water Show

has occurred annually on the shore of Lake Michigan

since 1959. This free event usually features daredevil

pilots, the U. S. Army Golden Knights, the U. S. Navy

Blue Angels, and the U. S. Air Force Thunderbirds.

Soldier Field is now primarily a football stadium and since 1971 home of the Chicago Bears. The field opened in 1924 and serves as a memorial to American soldiers who have died in wars. The original stadium was altered in 2003-2004 and from the outside is said to have a modern looking saucer sitting atop of Greek columns.

From the north

The Chicago skyline from North Avenue beach highlights Streeterville and the Gold Coast. The John Hancock building frames the skyline on the left and Willis Tower is seen on the right.

From the west

Prominent buildings include the Willis Tower and to its right, the 311 S. Wacker Dr. office building, seen after dusk with a beautifully illuminated upper structure.

Create your own caption here: _____

The Streeterville Neighborhood in a view from Navy Pier.

Classic (from the Planetarium)

The classic skyline photographs are taken from Solidarity Drive, near the Planetarium. In the twilight view, the tallest

buildings include the AON building and the Trump Tower to its left. The daytime view includes the Shedd Aquarium on

the left side of the photo and Willis Tower to its right.

Chicago at Twilight

This twilight skyline is dominated by the Willis Tower, AON Building, and Trump Tower.

One can also see Pritzker Pavilion in Millennium Park, beautifully illuminated by orange lights.

Credits and acknowledgments

Bruce Komiske, chief of new hospital construction, Ann & Robert H. Lurie Children's Hospital of Chicago, who led the way to the concept of whimsical images for identifying hospital floors.

The new hospital design and construction staff with Mitchell Associates, Inc. who did the signage design for the new hospital and displayed wonderful creativity in the creation of some of the whimsical images displayed in the hospital.

John Rabias, Photoshop guru, who introduced me to Photoshop and accomplished the impossible, making this collection of images possible.

Jen Freehill of Photocraft (Boulder, Colorado) who did all of the photo finishing to make the images jump off the pages.

Bobbye Cochran, one of Chicago's best graphic designers, who designed the trademark for Chicago Unleashed and designed our first book, *Whimsical Images of the Ann & Robert H. Lurie Children's Hospital of Chicago.*

Lesley Wallerstein, intellectual property attorney, who filed for trademarks, copyrights and image permissions.

Megan Brill, for caption suggestions.

Josh Arends, photographer

Alan Shortall Studios

Steve Turner, CEO, Origin Safaris (Nairobi, Kenya); Peter Leich, safari guide, Origin Safaris, and Gerry Koller, safari photo assistant.

Dave Brunner, computer hardware and software consultant.

Gary and Michelle Rich, who introduced me to the Chicago Lighthouse and its CEO, Dr. Janet Szlyk.

Jill Kongabel and Sam Assefa, who introduced me to Access Living and its CEO, Marca Bristo.

Chief Chicago Bridge Tender, City of Chicago.

Our human models: The crew of Chicago's First Lady river tour boat, coachmen for Chicago Horse and Carriage, Sandy and Margie Mintz, Todd Main, Sara Main, Aria and Chloe Wozniak, Eric Bolden, Adrian Simionou, Shawn, Emmy and Ally Peek, (Bill Jurek with Lincoln, Maureen Reid with Promise, Katie Howe and Greg Polman with Reuben, Chicago Lighthouse), Evelyn Rodriguez (Access Living).

Our animal models: Orangutans and gorillas at Tropic World, Brookfield Zoo; one day old chicks, with the help of Tim Christakos, senior exhibit specialist, the Museum of Science and Industry in Chicago; Rabbit from Red Door Animal Shelter, Black Bears from Vince Shute bear sanctuary, Minnesota; Sadie the cat (Meme and Gary Hopmayer), Knute the Dalmatian (Karen and Jim Gleeson); Cyrano, a green winged macaw raised by Tina Usher (The Parrot's Perch).

Harvey Stearn, Sedona, AZ, who introduced me to Carol Haralson, our award-winning book designer.

Page 23: Calder's "Flamingo," © 2014 Calder Foundation, New York / Artists Rights Society (ARS), New York

Page 27: Yaacov Agam's "Communication X9," © 2014 Artists Rights Society (ARS), New York / ADAGP, Paris

Page 41: Dubuffet's "Monument with Standing Beast," © 2014 Artists Rights Society (ARS), New York / ADAGP, Paris

Pages 108,109,110: Plensa's "Crown Fountain," © 2014 Artists Rights Society (ARS), New York / VEGAP, Madrid

All proceeds from sale of *Chicago Unleashed* will be donated by the book's publisher, Larry Broutman Photography, LLC, to two Chicago-based not-for-profit service agencies:

Chicago Lighthouse, committed to providing the highest quality educational, clinical, vocational, and rehabilitation services for children, youth, and adults who are blind or visually impaired, including deaf-blind and multi-disabled. For over 100 years, the Lighthouse has opened the doors of opportunity for people who are blind or visually impaired.

Access Living, established in 1980 as a change agent committed to fostering an inclusive society that enables Chicagoans with disabilities to live fully engaged and self-directed lives. Nationally recognized as a leading force in the disability advocacy community, Access Living challenges stereotypes, protects civil rights, and champions social reform.